EGGS-TRAORDINARY EASTER

Andy Robb

Eggs-traordinary Easter

Copyright © 2006 John Hunt Publishing Ltd
The Bothy, Deershot Lodge, Park Lane, Ropley, Hants, SO24 0BE, UK
E-mail: office@johnhunt-publishing.com
www.johnhunt-publishing.com
www.o-books.net

Text: © 2006 Andy Robb
Illustrations © 2006 Andy Robb
Page layout by Andy Robb
Design by BookDesign™, UK

ISBN 1 842981 67 6

Scriptures quoted from the Good News Bible published by The Bible
Societies/HarperCollins Publishers Ltd., UK

A CIP catalogue record for this book is available from the British Library.

Printed in Singapore by TWP

CONTENTS

Titles in the Boring Bible series;

Ballistic Beginnings

Bible Buster

The Big Boss

Catastrophic Kings

Crackers Christmas

Crazy Christians

Eggs-traordinary Easter

Hotchpotch Hebrews

Hyper Holy Happenings

Magnificent Moses

Saints Alive

Super Son

If I asked you what's the most important date on your calendar the chances are you'd say...

Thought you might.

Just thought it would be nice to involve you, that's all.
This Boring Bible book is gonna be *really* boring if all you get is me talking (or should I say *writing*) all the time. A bit of good old-fashioned audience participation should keep your interest.

Right, here's *another* question for you.
If I were to ask you what you think the most **important date**
in the whole of *history* was, what would your answer be?
And don't say your birthday again.

Nice try but think again.

Okay, Let me help you. Here's a whopper of a clue.

It's not Christmas!

Now take your time, I don't want to be accused of pressurising you.
Any ideas?
Does eggs, bunnies and hot cross buns ring any bells?

You're all just being **plain silly**.
Well, if you can't work it out then I'll just have to tell you. It's...

Er, that's not *quite* what I was going to say.
What I'd *intended* to tell you was that the answer's **Easter**.
I *definitely* wasn't planning to give **centre stage** to a bunny rabbit, *that's* for sure!

Nope!
In fact you couldn't be *wronger* (if that's a word).

No it's not. Improve your grammar pronto. This book is meant to be educational- The Editor.

I'll do my best. Now where was I before I was rudely interrupted? Oh yes, the Easter Bunny or should I say *Easter* but definitely **no bunny**.

Not at all, in fact I'm quite partial to **rabbit stew**.
Anyway, back to the question.

What do *I* reckon is the most important date in the whole of history? Well if you hadn't worked it out already the answer's... **Easter**.

If you want to know *why* I think that, then you're just gonna have to keep reading.

This Boring Bible book dives headfirst into everything you'll probably need to know about that time of year when people give each other **chocolate eggs** and when a rather annoying but, admitedly, **very cute** creature tries to steal the limelight.

I'd watch those **double negatives** if I were you, even if you *are* only a rabbit. That editor's a stickler for those sort of gaffs.

Okay, so I'll give you the fact that you're sort of endearing but that still doesn't make you particularly *relevant* to Easter.

In fact, howzabout we check out what all this Easter Bunny stuff is **right now** so we can then move on to more important things.

THE EASTER BUNNY

EXPOSED!

If you think the **Easter Bunny** is a modern invention then **think again**! We've got the ancient Anglo Saxons to thank (if that's the right word) for a floppy-eared animal getting the **star treatment**.

They worshipped the pagan goddess, **Eastre** who was symbolised by guess what? Yep, you got it...a **rabbit** (well actually it started out as a hare but 'cos there were more rabbits around things sort of got changed along the way).

So when and where did the cute little bunny get linked in with the Easter that we know and love?

Almost certainly in **Germany** sometime in the **1500's**.

The good old Germans can *also* take the credit for making the **world's first edible Easter bunnies** during the early 1800's. They hadn't quite got around to doing chocolate ones so it was scrummy **pastry and sugar bunnies** instead.

(Well, *sort of* scrummy if you prefer pastry to chocolate!).

During the **1700s** the Easter Bunny **packed his bags** and headed for **America** (along with a bunch of settlers from Germany) who took their Easter traditions with them to a place called Pennsylvania.

'**Oschter Haws**' as he was known, became a hot favourite with the kids in those days, second only to Santa Claus (or should I say, 'Kris Kringle' - see Boring Bible book *Crackers Christmas* for the full lowdown) and here's why.

They believed that if they were good, the Oschter Haws would lay a nest of **brightly coloured eggs**!

Two itty bitty problems!

Problem one: The Easter Bunny was supposed to be a **male** and as we all know (or *should* know) **men don't have babies**!

IN WHICH CASE IT LOOKS LIKE I'M GOING TO NEED TO GO ON A DIET!

Problem two: Rabbits don't lay eggs. They're mammals. Get your biology right kids!

But none of that seemed to deter them.

The children would build a **nest** in a secluded place in the home, the barn or the garden. Boys would use their **caps** and girls their **bonnets** to make the nests.

And *that's* where we get the use of elaborate **Easter baskets** from.

Right, now we've cleared up all that Easter Bunny stuff it's time to get stuck into all the *really* important business to do with Easter.

And because these books are called **Boring Bible** I'll bet you can't guess where we're going to get most of our Easter info...

Hey, how did you work *that* one out?

Well, now that the cats out of the bag and you all know that we're gonna be **raiding the Bible** for our Easter stuff I suppose I'd better tell *how* we're going to do it.

First off, if you're looking for the word 'Easter' in the Bible then you might as well **forget it**. Easter doesn't get a mention, well not in so many words.

What you *do* get is loads of stuff that tells you why what *we call* **Easter** is the most **important event** in the entire history of planet earth.

In fact, that's why this book's called ***Eggs-traordinary*** *Easter*, 'cos, as you're about to find out, some amazing and extraordinary things happened at Easter time around **2,000 years ago** - things that could change your life for ever.

And just in case you're worried that checking out stuff from the Bible is gonna be **mind-numbingly**, **brain-achingly boring** then let me tell you that the Bible is, without doubt, the most *un*-boring book you could ever wish to read.

IS UN-BORING A WORD?

The Author

No it's not! I've warned you about bad grammar already - The Editor.

Some *Un*-boring Bible Bits About Easter - Number One....

THE ROAD TO RUIN!

'**Jesus** and his **disciples** were now on the road going up to **Jerusalem**. Jesus was going ahead of the disciples, who were filled with alarm; the people who followed by were afraid. Once again Jesus took the twelve disciples aside and spoke of the things that were going to happen to him.'

> LISTEN, WE ARE GOING UP TO JERUSALEM WHERE THE SON OF MAN WILL BE HANDED OVER TO THE CHIEF PRIESTS AND THE TEACHERS OF THE LAW. THEY WILL CONDEMN HIM TO DEATH AND THEN HAND HIM OVER TO THE GENTILES, WHO WILL MOCK HIM, SPIT ON HIM, WHIP HIM AND KILL HIM, BUT THREE DAYS LATER HE WILL RISE TO LIFE.

A snatch from Bible book **Mark**, chapter 10 and verses 32 to 34.

Well, that's your *first un*-boring taster of Easter taken from the
the **world's best-selling book**, the Bible.
What d'you reckon?

NOT EXACTLY WHAT YOU'D CALL CHEERY, IS IT?

I hope you weren't expecting **cute little bunnies** after all
we've talked about?

WELL, NOW YOU MENTION IT...

When I want
your opinion I'll
ask for it, okay?

Actually, come to think of it, the *next* Bible bit we've lined up
for you does feature a **donkey,** if it's cute animals you want.
Roll the titles, it's time for another chunk of **Easter stuff** from
the extremely *un*-boring Bible.

Some *Un*-boring Bible Bits About Easter - Number Two....

THE BIG ENTRY!

'As they approached **Jerusalem**, near the towns of Bethphage and Bethany, they came to the **Mount of Olives**. Jesus sent two of his disciples on ahead with these instructions: "Go to the village there ahead of you. As soon as you get there, you will find a colt tied up that has never been ridden. Untie it and bring it here. And if someone asks you why you are doing that, tell him that the **Master** needs it and will send it back at once." So they went and found a colt out in the street, tied to the door of a house. As they were untying it, some of the bystanders asked them...

They answered just as Jesus had told them, and the bystanders let them go. They brought the colt to **Jesus**, threw their cloaks over the animal, and Jesus got on. Many people spread their cloaks on the road, while others cut **branches** in the fields and spread them on the road. The people who were in front and those who followed behind began to shout...

Jesus entered **Jerusalem**, went into the **Temple**, and looked round at everything. But since it was already late in the day, he went out to Bethany with the twelve disciples.'

A snatch from Bible book **Mark**, chapter 11 and verses 1 to 11.

Fire away.

Technically that's *two* questions but I'll answer you anyway.

Tell, you what, I'll go one better than answer your questions...

Before we head back to those old news reports (okay, so they're just made up, I admit it) let me tell you that when **Adam** and **Eve** disobeyed God right back at the **beginning of the world** they not only blew it for *themselves* but they also fouled it up (big time) for **you and me** as *well*.

It was like Adam and Eve had gone and built an **invisible wall** between human beings and God and nobody seemed to be able to tear it down.

Okay, so often people tried to forget that the wall was there...

But not for long.

In fact, **God** had a rather clever (if somewhat messy) way of reminding a bunch of people called the **Israelites** (check out Boring Bible book *Hotchpotch Hebrews*) that this **invisible barrier** wasn't going to budge, well not *yet*, anyway!
Back to our reporter at the scene...

It looks to me like God was mighty keen to **patch things up** between himself and us human beings but those animal sacrifices didn't seem to be much more than a **temporary fix**. So, what we're after is something (or some*one*) who's gonna get rid of that wall between us and God **once and for all**.

Let's go back to our intrepid TV reporter to see where he's surfaced this time...

And if you hadn't worked it out already the **saviour** they were talking about who'd just been born in Bethlehem was none other than **Jesus** as featured in the Christmas story.

For *more* Christmassy-type-stuff, get your hands on a copy of Boring Bible book *Crackers Christmas*.

Did You Know?   That Jesus's name actually means '**saviour**'.

Simple, it's someone who **saves you from something**.
That wasn't too difficult was it?

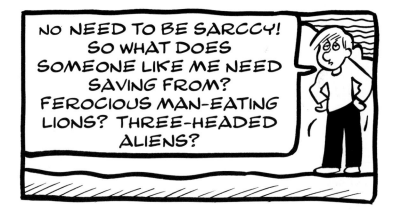

Who's being sarccy *now*?
No, it's nothing like that. Like I said earlier, there's a sort of
invisible wall that gets between people and God. What's that
wall made of? Nope it's not bricks, it's something called...

What's 'sin'?

Easy. It's all the bad stuff that us humans do like **lying** and **cheating** and **stealing** and **hating** and **not caring** and **holding grudges** and **not respecting our mum and dad** and **being greedy** and **selfish** and **swearing** and **grumbling** and **gossiping** and **doing what we want** and **getting too big for our boots** and **thinking we don't need God**.

That sort of thing.

Now what was that question you asked way back on page 20?

WHY WAS JESUS HEADING FOR JERUSALEM AND IF HE KNEW HE WAS FOR THE CHOP, WHY DIDN'T HE JUST HOT FOOT IT BACK THE WAY HE'D COME?

Oh yes. Right, now here's your answer.

It's because **Jesus** was the man who was going to sort *out* this sin problem, **once and for all**.

Jesus wasn't headed for Jerusalem for a nice day trip to Israel's capital city. No way!

Jesus was on a **mission from God** to **save the world**!

And *Jerusalem* was where the action was gonna take place.

Which I think is our cue to dive into...

Some *Un*-boring Bible Bits About Easter - Number Three....

WHIFF TIFF!

'It was now two days before the Festival of Passover and Unleavened Bread. The **chief priests** and the **teachers of the Law** were looking for a way to arrest Jesus secretly and **put him to death**. "We must not do it during the festival," they said, "or the people might riot."

Jesus was in Bethany at the house of Simon, a man who had suffered from a dreaded skin disease. While Jesus was eating, a woman came in with an **alabaster jar** full of a very **expensive perfume** made of pure nard.

She broke the jar and poured the perfume on Jesus' head. Some of the people there became angry and said to one another...

WHAT WAS THE USE OF WASTING THE PERFUME? IT COULD HAVE BEEN SOLD FOR MORE THAN THREE HUNDRED SILVER COINS AND THE MONEY GIVEN TO THE POOR!

And they criticized her harshly.
But Jesus said...

Then **Judas Iscariot**, one of the twelve disciples, went off to the chief priests in order to **betray Jesus** to them. They were pleased to hear what he had to say, and promised to give him money. So Judas started looking for a good chance to hand Jesus over to them.'

A snatch from Bible book **Mark**, chapter 14 and verses 1 to 11.

Some *Un*-boring Bible Bits About Easter - Number Four....

FAREWELL FEAST!

'On the first day of the **Festival of Unleavened Bread**, the day the lambs for the **Passover meal** were killed, Jesus' disciples asked him, "Where do you want us to go and get the Passover meal ready for you?"

Then **Jesus** sent two of them with these instructions...

> GO INTO THE CITY, AND A MAN CARRYING A JAR OF WATER WILL MEET YOU. FOLLOW HIM TO THE HOUSE HE ENTERS, AND SAY TO THE OWNER OF THE HOUSE: 'THE TEACHER SAYS, WHERE IS THE ROOM WHERE MY DISCIPLES AND I WILL EAT THE PASSOVER MEAL?' THEN HE WILL SHOW YOU A LARGE UPSTAIRS ROOM, PREPARED AND FURNISHED, WHERE YOU WILL GET EVERYTHING READY FOR US.

The disciples left, went to the city, and found everything just as Jesus had told them; and they prepared the Passover meal.

When it was evening, Jesus came with the twelve disciples.
While they were at the table eating, Jesus said...

The disciples were upset and began to ask him, one after the
other, "Surely you don't mean me, do you?"
Jesus answered, "It will be one of you twelve, one who dips his
bread in the dish with me. **The Son of Man will die as the
Scriptures say he will**; but how terrible for that man who
betrays the Son of Man! It would have been better for that man
if he had never been born!"
While they were eating, Jesus took **a piece of bread**, gave a
prayer of thanks, broke it, and gave it to his disciples.
"Take it," he said, "**this is my body**."
Then he took **a cup**, gave thanks to God, and
handed it to them; and they all drank from
it. Jesus said, "This is **my blood which is
poured out for many**, my blood which
seals God's covenant.
I tell you, I will never again drink this wine
until the day I drink the new wine in the
Kingdom of God."
Then they sang a hymn and went out to the Mount of Olives.'

A snatch from Bible book **Mark**, chapter 14 and verses
12 to 26.

Time for a break, I think.

If you know *anything* about Easter you'll know that before everyone gets around to **stuffing their faces with chocolate** and making themselves sick, you've got good old pancake day to keep your stomach happy.

What's *that* all about?

Here's what!

The History of the Pancake

Pancake Day (or Shrove Tuesday as it's *also* called) is the traditional feast day just before the beginning of **Lent** (which kicks off the next day, on Ash Wednesday).

Lent is the **40 days** that lead up to Easter and is traditionally a time of when people **fast** (go without food or at the very least they cut out treats) as they get themselves ready for Easter.

On Shrove Tuesday Christians went to confession and were "shriven" (forgiven of their sins).

It was *also* their last chance to use **eggs and fats** before getting stuck into their Lent fast.

And guess what you can make *out* of eggs and fats?

Yep, you got it...**pancakes**!

Pancakes aren't some **new-fangled invention**. The pancake recipe appeared in cookbooks as far back as **1439**. (And no, you parents *won't* remember that far back so don't be tempted to ask them!).

And it wouldn't be Pancake Day without having a go at tossing (or flipping) your flat disc of fried batter. In fact, just so's you don't make a *complete* fool of yourself, here's a bit of handy help.

The Boring Bible Guide to Tossing a Pancake

1. Cook a pancake(obvious but essential). Make sure your pancake isn't *too* big or be prepared to suffer the embarrassing consequences when you attempt to toss it...

2. Be certain to cook your pancake on *both* sides before commencing **big-time tossing**. A gentle flip with a spatula will enable you to cook the other side...

I said *gentle*, didn't I?

3. You're now ready to toss your pancake. Some basic rules.

a) The pancake has got to land back in your frying pan. It's no good just tossing it as hard as you can and then forgetting about it. You might be *tempted* to see if you can enter the record books by launching the world's first **batter-lite** (batter satellite) but **resist it**!

b) Be aware of onlookers when tossing. A frying pan is a **dangerous weapon** if not used carefully. The aim *isn't* to see how many bystanders you can give concussion with one flip of your frying pan.

c) Don't try and be clever and catch somebody else's pancake. That's just **plain silly**.

4. Hold the frying pan **loosely** (wrist flexibility is vital) but **firmly** (you'll look a silly sausage if you drop it).

With the elbow of your holding arm bent, your legs slightly apart and your gaze fixed squarely on your pancake, flick the frying pan with both strength and determination. As the pancake launches skyward do not take you eyes off it for one instant, continuing to track its course as it flips over in mid air and then gracefully decends to earth.

Your frying pan should (if all goes to plan) be ready and waiting to collect the pancake on its return.

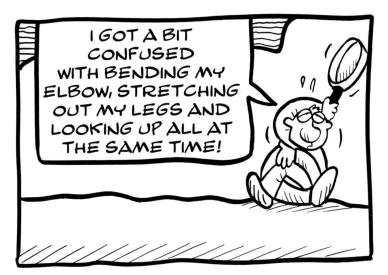

Fascinating Fact:

The world's biggest pancake was cooked in Rochdale, England in 1994. It was an amazing 15 metres in diameter, weighed three tonnes and had an estimated two million calories.

If you've been paying attention (and if you haven't been, why not?) then you'll have noticed that a guy called **Judas Iscariot** was planning to do the dirty on Jesus by handing him over to the religious leaders (who hated Jesus) so that they could put on him trial for **claiming to be God's Son**.

Okay, so Jesus *was* God's Son but *they* didn't seem to think so, which made Jesus guilty (as far as *they* were concerned) of **blasphemy**.

Well, basically it's saying or doing stuff that insults God. Because Jesus *was* God it was hardly something he could be accused of, but that didn't seem to stop the religious leaders. They wanted Jesus out of the way, **pronto**, and if that meant being **killing him** then all the better.

Because Jesus was such a hit with the crowds they could never find the right moment to arrest him without causing a stir.

If they could only lay their hands him when nobody else was around then that would be perfect.

When Judas Iscariot came along and offered to do the job *for* them they were **over the moon**.

But what made one of Jesus's top team **turn traitor**?

Let's check out some stuff about Judas Iscariot to see what we can discover.

THE JUDAS FILES

Name: Judas Iscariot
Most Recent Job: Disciple of Jesus of Nazareth
Special Duties: He was in charge of their money
Brownie Points: He referred to Jesus as 'Rabbi' (or teacher)
Black Marks: He never referred to Jesus as 'Lord' (which the *other* disciples did)
Bad Moves: Judas gave a woman a hard time for pouring expensive perfume over Jesus's feet. Jesus stood up for the lady but Judas was miffed that so much money had been wasted (as far as *he* was concerned).

The chances are Judas was more annoyed that the money spent on the perfume hadn't been stashed away in the disciples' money bag - so that he could dip into it when nobody was looking, which is what the Bible tells us he did!

Just one of the perks of being treasurer was probably how *Judas* saw it.

Claims to Fame: Judas shopped Jesus to the religious leaders for 30 pieces of silver (a few hundred pounds in today's money).

What Made Him Tick?: Judas probably thought that Jesus was the man the Jewish nation had been waiting for, who was gonna free them from being ruled by those rotten Romans. When it became obvious to Judas that this wasn't on Jesus's 'To Do' list he wanted out.

What Became of Judas?: Judas realised that he'd made a big mistake betraying Jesus to the authorities.

When Judas realised that he couldn't persuade them to change their minds about arresting Jesus he handed back the silver pieces and went off and hanged himself.

What Can We Learn From Judas's Life?: Make sure you check out who Jesus really is before you start to fill your head with loads of wrong ideas about him.

(Boring Bible book *Super Son* will give you just about all the lowdown on Jesus that you'll need).

That's a very good question but I'm going to answer your question with *another* question.

If someone suddenly pops up out of the blue and announces...

Or perhaps somebody else says...

What would you think of them?

Nor me.

If somebody's gonna stand up and tell everyone that they're **someone special sent from God** then you're going to want to have a bit of **proof** that they *are* who they claim to *be*.

What we've got to look for is something that backs up their claim, such as a bit of **advance warning** that they're on their way.

Something like that would be *really* handy.

It should therefore be no surprise to you that that's *exactly* what **God** lined up for **Jesus** before his Son paid a visit to Planet Earth. The Bible calls them **prophecies** but because they sort of **advertised** that Jesus was on his way then that's what *we're* gonna stick with.

Now turn the page and see for yourself.

THE BORING BIBLE
CLASSIFIED ADS

Births:

A virgin who is pregnant will have a son and will name him Immanuel (which means 'God is with us').

For further details please contact Bible book Isaiah, chapter 7 and verse 14.

Coming Soon:

A voice cries out, "Prepare in the wilderness a road for our God! Clear the way in the desert for our God!"

Check out full details of this forthcoming event @ www.isaiah.40.3

Public Engagements:

Shout for joy you people of Jerusalem! Look your king is coming to you! He comes triumphant and victorious but humble and riding on a donkey, on a colt, the foal of a donkey.

As received from our Royal Correspondent Zechariah. Taken from Chapter 9, verse 9 of his most recent article.

Announcements:

The LORD has declared, 'You are my son, today I have become your father'.
With love and best wishes from Psalm 2 verse 7.

Deaths:

He was put to death for the sins of our people. He was placed in a grave with evil men. He was buried with the rich.

If you would like to know more about this sad occurrence then call in at Isaiah 53 and he will gladly share the full circumstances surrounding it.

Clothing:

They gamble for my clothes and divide them among themselves.

Reply to Bible book Psalms, chapter 22 and verse 18 for further information.

Now for the *interesting* bit.

Nope, but when you check out what happened to Jesus when he eventually turned up (hundreds of years *after* these ads were written) you'll have to agree that it's **awesomely fascinating**.

You're on! Let's take a look and see whether those **ads for Jesus** actually came true.

Births:
A virgin who is pregnant will have a son and will name him Immanuel (which means 'God is with us').
For further details please contact Bible book Isaiah, chapter 7 and verse 14.

'This was how the birth of **Jesus Christ** took place. His mother **Mary** was engaged to **Joseph** but before they were married she found out she was going to have a baby by the **Holy Spirit**. Joseph was a man who always did what was right but he did not want to disgrace Mary publicly so he made plans to break the engagement privately. While he was thinking about this, **an angel of the Lord** appeared to him in a dream and said...

JOSEPH, DESCENDANT OF DAVID, DO NOT BE AFRAID TO TAKE MARY TO BE YOUR WIFE. FOR IT IS BY THE HOLY SPIRIT THAT SHE HAS CONCEIVED. SHE WILL HAVE A SON AND YOU WILL NAME HIM JESUS BECAUSE HE WILL SAVE PEOPLE FROM THEIR SINS.

Now all this happened in order to make what the Lord had said through the prophet come true, "A virgin will become pregnant and have a son and he will be called Immanuel" (which means. 'God is with us').'

Check out Bible book **Matthew**, chapter 1 and read from verse 18 right through to verse 23.

Coming Soon:
A voice cries out, "Prepare in the wilderness a road for our God! Clear the way in the desert for our God!"
Check out full details of this forthcoming event @ www.isaiah.40.3

'At that time **John the Baptist** came to the desert of Judea and started preaching...

TURN AWAY FROM YOUR SINS BECAUSE THE KINGDOM OF HEAVEN IS NEAR!

John was the man the prophet **Isaiah** was talking about when he said, "Some is shouting in the desert, 'Prepare a road for the Lord; make a straight path for him to travel!' '

Check out Bible book **Matthew**, chapter 3 and read from verse 1 through to verse 3.

If you keep on reading you'll discover that John the Baptist was the warm up man for Jesus.

Public Engagements:

Shout for joy, you people of Jerusalem! Look, your king is coming to you! He comes triumphant and victorious, but humble and riding on a donkey, on a colt, the foal of a donkey.

As received from our Royal Correspondent Zechariah. Taken from Chapter 9, verse 9 of his most recent article.

'As **Jesus** and his disciples approached **Jerusalem**, they came to Bethphage at the Mount of Olives. There Jesus sent two of the disciples on ahead with these instructions...

GO TO THE VILLAGE THERE AHEAD OF YOU AND AT ONCE YOU WILL FIND A DONKEY TIED UP WITH HER COLT BESIDE HER. UNTIE THEM AND BRING THEM TO ME. AND IF ANYONE SAYS ANYTHING TELL HIM 'THE MASTER NEEDS THEM' AND HE WILL LET THEM GO AT ONCE.

This happened in order to make what the prophet had said come true: "Tell the city of Zion, look, your king is coming to you! He is humble and rides on a donkey, and on a colt, the foal of a donkey." '

Check out Bible book **Matthew**, chapter 21 and read from verse 1 through to verse 5.
(You've already read what happened *next* in this story on **page 19**, unless you've skipped some pages and if so, you're going to need a jolly good excuse!).

Announcements:
The LORD has declared,
'You are my son, today
I have become your father'.
With love and best wishes from
Psalm 2 verse 7.

'In the sixth month of Elizabeth's pregnancy God sent the **angel Gabriel** to a town in Galilee named **Nazareth**. He had a message for a girl promised in marriage to a man named Joseph, who was a descendant of King David. The girl's name was **Mary**.
The angel came to her and said...

Mary was deeply troubled by the angel's message and she wondered what his words meant. The angel said to her...'

Check out Bible book **Luke**, chapter 1 and read from verse 26 through to verse 32.

Deaths:
He was put to death for the sins of our people.
He was placed in a grave with evil men. He was buried with the rich.

If you would like to know more about this sad occurrence then call in at Isaiah 53 and he will gladly share the full circumstances surrounding it.

'When it was evening, a rich man from Arimathea arrived; his name was **Joseph** and he also was a disciple of Jesus. He went into the presence of **Pilate** and asked for the body of Jesus. Pilate gave orders for the body to be given to Joseph. So he took it, wrapped it in a new linen sheet and placed it in his own **tomb** which he had just recently dug out of a solid rock. The he rolled a large stone across the entrance to the tomb and went away.'

Check out Bible book **Matthew**, chapter 27 and read from verse 57 through to verse 60.

(Just for your info, this was stuff that happened shortly after Jesus had been executed by the Romans)

Clothing:
They gamble for my clothes and divide them among themselves.

Reply to Bible book Psalms, chapter 22 and verse 18 for further information.

'After the soldiers had crucified **Jesus** they took his clothes and divided them into four parts, one for each **soldier**.

They took his **robe**, which was made of one piece of woven cloth without any seams in it.

The soldiers said to one another...

LET'S NOT TEAR IT. LET'S THROW DICE TO SEE WHO WILL GET IT.

This happened in order to make the scripture come true: "They divided my clothes among themselves and gambled for my robe."

And this is what the soldiers did.'

Check out Bible book **John**, chapter 19 and read verses 23 and 24.

Fascinating Fact:

It's reckoned you can find hundreds of prophecies (or ads) that talk about Jesus before he actually visited this planet.
Some of them are really easy to understand and others need a bit more brain power.
Either way you can't get away from the very fascinating fact that Jesus was advertised before he arrived so that we wouldn't be left in any doubt who he really is (God's Son).

HANG ON A MINUTE! THAT'S ALL VERY INTERESTING BUT ANY CHANCE OF TELLING US HOW THEY RECEIVED THESE PROPHECY THINGIES!

Good question.

First off, there's some things that you need to get into your head about **God** such as the fact that God doesn't actually live in **time** like you and me.

God doesn't ever suffer from one of those horrible I-don't-want to-go-school Monday morning feelings 'cos in heaven (where God lives) they don't *have* days of the week.

And **God** doesn't have to to worry about dying (sorry to be morbid)...

...'cos in heaven **everyone lives for ever**.

Which means that God can look at the world (from outside of time) and see what's *been* happening, what's happening right *now* and even what's *going* to happen in the future.

Cool or what?

God could see **everything** that was going to happen to **Jesus** *before* it happened and now all God needed was somebody (or some*bodies*) to tell it to.

Enter the **prophets**...

The prophets were a bit like **satellite dishes** that people stick on their houses to receive TV signals,,,

I said 'a bit *like*' not actually *fitted* to a house!
Prophets were people who **listened out** for things that God was saying (in the same way that a satellite dish picks up TV signals) and then passed the info on.

The Bible's *full* of stuff that these prophets got first hand from God because (fortunately for us) they had the good sense to **write it down**.

The messages (or prophecies) came in *all* shapes and sizes.

Some were **warnings** not to do this or that.

Some were **encouraging** people when they were feeling a bit down in the dumps.

And *some* were **advertising** things that were going to happen in the future (like Jesus visting this planet).

If you want to check out a bit *more* about these prophets (and there were *heaps* of 'em) then it might be worth parting with a bit of your cash and buying a copy of Boring Bible book *Catastrophic Kings*.

Alternatively, you could just keep your knowledge of the prophets to the **bare minimum**.

Some *Un*-boring Bible Bits About Easter - Number Five....

GARDEN TRAP!

'They came to a place called **Gethsemane**, and Jesus said to his disciples, "Sit here while I pray." He took Peter, James, and John with him. **Distress and anguish** came over him, and he said to them, "The sorrow in my heart is so great that it almost crushes me. Stay here and keep watch."
He went a little farther on, threw himself on the ground, and prayed that, if possible, he might not have to go through that time of suffering...

Then he returned and found the three disciples **asleep**. He said to Peter, "Simon, are you asleep? Weren't you able to stay awake even for one *hour*?" And he said to them, "Keep watch, and pray that you will not fall into temptation. The spirit is willing, but the flesh is weak."

He went away once more and prayed, saying the same words. Then he came back to the disciples and found them asleep; they could not keep their eyes open.

And they did not know what to say to him.

When he came back the *third* time, he said to them, "Are you *still* sleeping and resting? Enough! The hour has come! Look, the **Son of Man** is now being handed over to the power of sinners. Get up, let us go. Look, here is the man who is betraying me!" Jesus was still speaking when **Judas**, one of the twelve disciples, arrived.

With him was a crowd armed with **swords and clubs**, and sent by the chief priests, the teachers of the Law, and the elders. The traitor had given the crowd a signal: "The man I kiss is the one you want. Arrest him and take him away under guard." As soon as Judas arrived, he went up to Jesus and said...

...and kissed him.

So they **arrested Jesus** and held him tight. But one of those standing there drew his sword and struck at the High Priest's slave, cutting off his ear. Then Jesus spoke up and said to them, "Did you have to come with swords and clubs to capture me, as though I were an outlaw? Day after day I was with you teaching in the Temple, and you did not arrest me. But the Scriptures must come true." Then all the disciples left him and ran away. '

A snatch from Bible book **Mark**, chapter 14 and verses 32 to 50.

Some *Un*-boring Bible Bits About Easter - Number Six....

ON TRIAL!

'Then **Jesus** was taken to the **High Priest's house**, where all the chief priests, the elders, and the teachers of the Law were gathering.

Peter followed from a distance and went into the **courtyard** of the High Priest's house. There he sat down with the guards, keeping himself warm by the fire.

The chief priests and the whole Council tried to find some evidence against Jesus in order to put him to death, but they could not find *any*.

Many witnesses told lies against Jesus, but their stories did not agree.

Then some men stood up and told this lie against Jesus...

WE HEARD HIM SAY, 'I WILL TEAR DOWN THIS TEMPLE WHICH MEN HAVE MADE, AND AFTER THREE DAYS I WILL BUILD ONE THAT IS NOT MADE BY MEN.

Not even they, however, could make their stories agree.

The High Priest stood up in front of them all and questioned Jesus, "Have you no answer to the accusation they bring against you?"

But Jesus **kept quiet** and would not say a word. *Again* the High Priest questioned him, "Are you the Messiah, the Son of the Blessed God?"

"The High Priest tore his robes and said, "We don't need any more witnesses! You heard his blasphemy. What is your decision?"

They all voted against him: **he was guilty and should be put to death**.

Some of them began to **spit** on Jesus, and they **blindfolded him and hit him**. "Guess who hit you!" they said.

And the guards took him and **slapped him**.'

A snatch from Bible book **Mark**, chapter 14 and verses 53 to 65.

If you've been reading this book non-stop (and even if you *haven't*) I think it's time you took some exercise before you turn into a **couch potato**.

Flex you pingies (or fingers if you're an older reader) and flick through the pages of this wonderfully educational and entertaining book until you reach **page 36** and **37**.

Hold your horses! Don't go yet! You need to know *why* you're heading there first.

Right, when you arrive, after having given you're pingies (or fingers) a **mini work-out** have a quick glance at this double page spread and check out what's occurring.

When you think you've downloaded all the info your brain can hold, return to this page and we can continue.

A picture of me sitting around, waiting for you to come back.

All done? Then we can move on!

One word that crops up more than once on those pages is ...

Yep, well observed! Have a gold star!

But what exactly *is* **Passover** and what on *earth* has it got to do with **Easter**?

Thanks for the invitation, I *will*!

Passover Facts

Passover (or the **Festival of Unleavened Bread**) celebrates the Jewish nation's rather spectacular escape from slavery in **Egypt** (thousands of years ago).

The **Israelites** (as they were *also* known) had been held captive for centuries but God had heard their cries for help and had sent a man called **Moses** to do the job of freeing them from the clutches of the **terrible Egyptian Pharaoh**.

(Full details in Boring Bible book *Magnificent Moses*).

The long and short of it was that there was **no way on this earth** that Pharaoh was gonna let his slave workforce go free. Not even a bunch of horrid plagues could seem to change his stubborn mind.

But when God sent an **angel** to **kill every firstborn Egyptian**, Pharaoh backed down.

To prevent the angel of God mistakenly killing any *Israelites*, God instructed them to daub the door frames of their houses with **lambs blood** as a sign for the angel to...**pass over**!

And because the Israelites had to make a **quick exit** (in case the Pharaoh changed his mind, which he did, but that's another story) they didn't have time to prepare their daily **bread** supplies.

The bread they hastily stashed away to take with them was **unleavened** (it didn't have yeast in it to make it rise).

And to make **100% certain** the Israelites never, *ever* forgot how they'd been rescued by God, he told them that, once a year, they had to have a special **Passover meal** which included some **unleavened bread** and **lamb**.

Did You Know?

The Festival of Passover lasts for eight days. The highlight is the seder, a colourful ceremony generally celebrated during the first two nights of Passover. At the seder the family gathers together and the story of the Exodus from Egypt is retold.

Don't rush me! I was *getting* to that bit.

As I've already told you, Jesus was completely up to speed with what was going to happen to him when he turned up in **Jerusalem** (he was going to get executed, in case you'd forgotten).

We've *also* checked out how the Israelites had to sacrifice **lambs** (and other animals) to cover over their sins.

Now *here's* where the link comes - and it's **clever**!

Jesus was going to allow *himself* to be **sacrificed** (killed) to **take the punishment** for everybody's sins who's *ever* lived. ('Cos Jesus was God and he'd never done anything wrong that made him a **perfect sacrifice** - *precisely* what God was looking for).

When Jesus drunk the **red wine** with his disciples at the Passover meal he told them that *this* time it was going to be *his* blood that was going to be shed so that God would **pass over** our sin.

It's like we avoid getting punished by God because of the **blood**. Is that good or what?

And the **bread** represented Jesus's **body** that he was going to allow to be nailed to a wooden cross so *he* could take the punishment for all the stuff *we've* done wrong.

Between you and me I don't think that Jesus's disciples had a *clue* what he was talking about when he said those things but because *we* do then there's not really much excuse for us if we completely ignore it and pretend it didn't happen.

More about that *later*.

But now it's time for this...

Easter Eggs Eggs-plained

Using an **egg** to celebrate something (like we do at Easter) is not a new phenomenon. If you travel back in time (which you can't so you'll just have to use your imagination) you'll discover that the egg was a symbol of **rebirth** in most cultures.

Eggs were often wrapped in gold leaf or (if you were a peasant) coloured brightly by boiling them with the leaves or petals of certain flowers.

The **Egyptians** buried eggs in their tombs.

The **Greeks** placed eggs on the top of graves...

AND THE BRITISH PLACED THEM IN EGG CUPS WHICH IS MUCH MORE SENSIBLE!

Eggs were also given as gifts by the ancient Greeks, Persians, and Chinese at their spring festivals.

All in all the humble egg appears to have been quite well thought of through the ages.

In some parts of **Germany** (during the early 1880s) Easter eggs were substituted for **birth certificates**!

First off, the egg was coloured with dye. Then a design (which included the baby's name and birth date) was etched into the shell with a needle or sharp tool. Amazingly these rather unusual birth certificates were acceptable legal evidence of identity and age. How odd!

Decorating and colouring eggs for Easter was also the custom in **England** during the middle ages. The household accounts of Edward I (for the year 1290) recorded an outlay of eighteen pence for **four hundred and fifty eggs** which were to be covered with gold and coloured as Easter prezzies.

Here's a question for you.

What's the most money you'd part with to buy an Easter egg?

50p?

£2.50?

£5.00?

£10.00?

Well, if you picked the *last* option you're still a **million miles away** from the sort of dosh you'd need for you to get your hands on a world-famous **Faberge egg**.

(And by the way, if you opted for just 50p then you should be ashamed of yourself for being such a **meanie**!).

Faberge Eggs (the world's most valuable eggs) were hand-crafted in the **1880s** by the great goldsmith **Peter Carl Faberge**, and were commissioned by **Czar Alexander III of Russia** as gifts for his wife, Czarina Maria Feodorovna.

The first Faberge egg measured two and a half inches long and had a deceptively simple exterior.

But inside the white enamel shell was a golden yolk which, when opened, revealed a gold hen with ruby eyes.

Not only that but the hen could be opened by lifting the beak to reveal a tiny diamond replica of the imperial crown.

Fascinating Fact:

Faberge eggs have regularly sold for millions of dollars and even as much as 9.6 million.

LOOKS LIKE I'LL JUST HAVE TO HANG ON TO MY SOP THEN!

Now back to our *un*-boring Bible bits...

Some *Un*-boring Bible Bits About Easter - Number Seven....

DEATH SENTENCE!

'Early in the morning the **chief priests** met hurriedly with the elders, the teachers of the Law, and the whole Council, and made their plans. They put **Jesus** in chains, led him away, and handed him over to **Pilate**. Pilate questioned him...

The chief priests were accusing Jesus of many things, so Pilate questioned him again, "Aren't you going to *answer*? Listen to all their accusations!"
Again Jesus **refused to say a word**, and Pilate was **amazed**.

At every Passover Festival Pilate was in the habit of setting free any **one prisoner** the people asked for.

At that time a man named **Barabbas** was in prison with the rebels who had committed murder in the riot.

When the crowd gathered and began to ask Pilate for the usual favour, he asked them...

He knew very well that the chief priests had handed Jesus over to him because they were **jealous**.

But the chief priests **stirred up the crowd** to ask, instead, for Pilate to set Barabbas free for them. Pilate spoke again to the crowd, "What, then, do you want me to do with the one you call the king of the Jews?"

They shouted back..

"But what crime has he committed?" Pilate asked.

They shouted all the louder, "Crucify him!"

Pilate wanted to please the crowd, so he set Barabbas free for them. Then he had Jesus whipped and handed him over to be crucified.'

A snatch from Bible book **Mark**, chapter 15 and verses 1 to 15.

Some *Un*-boring Bible Bits About Easter - Number Eight....

MOCKED!

'The soldiers took **Jesus** inside to the courtyard of the
governor's palace and called together the rest of the company.
They put a **purple robe** on Jesus, made a **crown out of
thorny branches**, and put it on his head. Then they began to
salute him...

They **beat him over the head** with a stick, **spat on him**, fell
on their knees, and **bowed down to him**.
When they had finished mocking him, they took off the purple
robe and put his own clothes back on him.
Then they led him out to **crucify him**.
On the way they met a man named Simon, who was coming
into the city from the country, and the soldiers forced him to
carry **Jesus' cross**.
(Simon was from Cyrene and was the father of Alexander and
Rufus.)
They took Jesus to a place called **Golgotha**, which means "The
Place of the Skull".

There they tried to give him wine mixed with a drug called myrrh, but Jesus would not drink it.

Then they **crucified him** and divided his clothes among themselves, throwing dice to see who would get which piece of clothing.

It was nine o'clock in the morning when they crucified him.

The notice of the accusation against him said: "The King of the Jews".

They also crucified two bandits with Jesus, one on his right and the other on his left.

People passing by shook their heads and **hurled insults** at Jesus...

In the same way the chief priests and the teachers of the Law jeered at Jesus, saying to each other, "He saved others, but he cannot save himself! Let us see the Messiah, the king of Israel, come down from the cross now, and we will believe in him!" And the two who were crucified with Jesus insulted him also.'

A snatch from Bible book **Mark**, chapter 15 and verses 16 to 32.

Did You Know?

That Romans didn't actually *invent* crucifixion as a method of execution even though it was something they spent a lot of time perfecting. It appears that the ancient **Persians** can take the credit (or blame) for thinking up this **terrible torture**.

A guy called **King Darius** (as featured in Bible book Daniel) had **3000 Babylonians** crucified in or around 519 B.C. Very gruesome!

Then a couple of hundred years later a young Greek fella called **Alexander the Great** (yep,

you've probably heard of him) *also* used crucifixion when he was out and about conquering other lands. In Tyre, alone, he put 2,000 citizens to death by crucifying them.

The **Romans** eventually conquered the **Greeks** and it was from them that the Romans probably learned crucifixion.

But before you start having a downer on the Romans let me tell you that they weren't alone in being fond of crucifying people as a punishment. Indians, Assyrians, Scythians, Celts, Germans and Britains *also* got in on the act!

Who was Roman crucifixion for?

Roman law usually spared Roman citizens from being crucified which meant that this horrific means of execution was reserved for the likes of rebels, foreigners, military enemies, violent criminals, robbers and slaves.

The Romans thought *nothing* of crucifying slaves and it was such a **common event** that crucifixion became known as the '**slaves' punishment**'...

To prove my point, the history books tell us that when the slave rebellion of **Spartacus** was crushed, the Roman general Crassus had **six thousand** of the slave prisoners **crucified** along a stretch of the **Appian Way** (which was the main road leading into Rome).

Hardly much fun for tourists who'd come to visit that great city.

So, what exactly happened when somebody was crucified?

Well, for starters, there wasn't *one* way of doing the dirty deed but I'll spare you the gory details save to say that the bottom line was making sure the person being executed was **thoroughly humiliated**.

A crucifixion generally began with a **flogging** (usually done by two soldiers) using a short whip of several leather thongs of different lengths. Tied to these leather thongs were small iron balls or sharp pieces of sheep bones. The victim was stripped of his clothing and his hands were tied above him to a post and he was flogged until he was half dead though some people did actually die from just the flogging.

Next up, the condemned man was forced to **carry his own cross** to the place where he was going to be crucified (outside the city walls).

Just for your info, this was not the *whole* cross but simply the **crossbeam** (or patibulum, if you're interested in a little latin).

I'M A LITTLE LATIN!

Even carrying just the crossbeam was no mean feat.
It could have weighed anything from **75 -125 pounds** which is
the weight of an **average pig**.

Round the victim's **neck** was hung a sign (or **titulus**-more latin
for you, isn't this book educational?) which said what the person
was guilty of.
The 'titulus' was then fixed to the top of the cross when they
arrived at the execution site.

To save time and for effeciency (for which the Romans were
rather famous) they often had **permanent places of
execution** outside cities where the upright beam of the cross
was already in position, ready and waiting for the crossbeam to
be attached to it.

At the execution site the victim had to be given (by law) a drink of wine mixed with myrrh (also known as **gall** - aren't you learning loads?) which acted as a mild pain killer.

The condemned man was stripped naked, thrown to the ground on his back with his arms outstretched along the crossbeam.

His hands were either **tied or nailed to the crossbeam** (but more often than not nailed) and then lifted up so that the crossbeam was attached to the upright beam.

Last, but not least, the victim's feet were nailed, one on top of the other, to the upright beam with another iron spike.

On the upright beam was a small block (**sedile**) which the crucified man could rest his weight on.

Fascinating Fact:

The Romans used two sorts of cross to execute criminals - a short cross (which was no more than seven feet tall) and a high cross.

When Jesus was crucified, one of the soldiers guarding him tried to give him a drink by putting a wet sponge on the end of a hyssop stalk. These stalks were only about 20 inches long so we're probably safe to assume that Jesus was hung on a short cross.

It's impossible to imagine the pain that a person being crucified would have experienced.

It was slow, it was agonising and it was terrible.

But what is even *more* incredible is that Jesus *chose* to allow himself to suffer like this for you and me.

Let's read more of the story...

Some *Un*-boring Bible Bits About Easter - Number Nine....

JESUS DIES!

'At noon the whole country was covered with **darkness**, which lasted for three hours. At three o'clock Jesus cried out with a loud shout, "Eloi, Eloi, lema sabachthani?" which means, "My God, my God, why did you abandon me?" Some of the people there heard him and said...

One of them ran up with a sponge, soaked it in cheap wine, and put it on the end of a stick. Then he held it up to Jesus' lips and said, "Wait! Let us see if Elijah is coming to bring him down from the cross!"

With a loud cry Jesus died.

The curtain hanging in the Temple was **torn in two,** from top to bottom. The army officer who was standing there in front of the cross saw how Jesus had died. "**This man was really the Son of God!**" he said.

Some women were there, looking on from a distance. Among them were Mary Magdalene, Mary the mother of the younger

James and of Joseph, and Salome. They had followed Jesus while he was in Galilee and had helped him. Many other women who had come to Jerusalem with him were there also.'

A snatch from Bible book **Mark**, chapter 15 and verses 33 to 41.

Well remembered.

Tell you what, how about checking out this *next* Bible bit to find out some interesting stuff that happened shortly *after* Jesus had been executed.

Just to set the scene, Jesus has been confirmed dead by the Romans and he's been **buried in a tomb**.

Three days have passed since Friday's crucifixion.

Some *Un*-boring Bible Bits About Easter - Number Ten....

WHERE'S JESUS?

'Early on **Sunday morning**, while it was still dark, **Mary Magdalene** went to the **tomb** and saw that the stone had been taken away from the entrance. She went running to **Simon Peter** and the other disciple, whom Jesus loved, and told them...

THEY HAVE TAKEN THE LORD FROM THE TOMB AND WE DON'T KNOW WHERE THEY HAVE PUT HIM!

Then Peter and the other disciple **went to the tomb**.
The two of them were **running**, but the other disciple ran faster than Peter and reached the tomb first.
He bent over and saw the linen wrappings, but he did not go in. Behind him came Simon Peter, and he went straight into the tomb. He saw the **linen wrappings lying there** and the **cloth which had been round Jesus' head**. It was not lying with the linen wrappings but was rolled up by itself. Then the other disciple, who had reached the tomb first, also went in; he saw and believed. (They still did not understand the scripture which said that he must rise from death.)
Then the disciples went back home.

Mary stood **crying** outside the tomb. While she was still crying, she bent over and looked in the tomb and saw **two angels** there dressed in white, sitting where the body of Jesus had been, one at the head and the other at the feet...

She answered, "They have taken my Lord away, and I do not know where they have put him!"

Then she turned round and saw Jesus standing there; but she did not know that it was Jesus...

She *thought* he was **the gardener**, so she said to him,
"If you took him away, sir, tell me where you have put him,
and I will go and get him."
Jesus said to her, "Mary!"
She turned towards him and said in Hebrew, "Rabboni!"
(This means "Teacher").

DO NOT HOLD ON TO ME BECAUSE I HAVE NOT YET GONE BACK UP TO THE FATHER. BUT GO TO MY BROTHERS AND TELL THEM THAT I AM RETURNING TO HIM WHO IS MY FATHER AND THEIR FATHER, AND MY GOD AND THEIR GOD.

So Mary Magdalene went and told the disciples that she had
seen the Lord and related to them what he had told her. '

A snatch from Bible book **John**, chapter 20 and verses 1 to 18.

After speeding through those Bible bits I'll bet you've got *loads* of questions that you want to ask, haven't you?

Which is why you're gonna get the chance to fire any question you want at the Boring Bible's **resident brainbox**, (no, it's not me but) **Professor Tanktop**.

ANOTHER TIP TOP QUESTION IF I SAY SO MYSELF!
THE TEMPLE WAS THE PLACE WHERE THE JEWISH PEOPLE WORSHIPPED GOD AND MADE SACRIFICES TO HIM. THE MOST SPECIAL AREA WAS CALLED THE HOLY OF HOLIES WHERE, ONCE A YEAR, A SPECIAL PRIEST WAS ALLOWED TO ENTER - HE WAS GOING INTO THE VERY PRESENCE OF GOD AND A GIGANTIC CURTAIN KEPT THE PLACE HIDDEN.
WITH SIN SORTED BY JESUS, GOD RIPPED THE CURTAIN IN TWO AS IF TO SAY THAT FROM NOW ON EVERYONE CAN COME INTO HIS PRESENCE, PROVIDING OF COURSE THAT THEY ACKNOWLEDGE WHAT JESUS HAS DONE FOR THEM.
TIME FOR ONE MORE.

WHY DID JESUS COME BACK TO LIFE AGAIN?

YES, UM, ER, JOLLY GOOD QUESTION AND I'M GLAD YOU ASKED. JESUS WAS RAISED BACK TO LIFE TO DEMONSTRATE THAT THE SIN HE'D CARRIED FOR US ON THE CROSS COULDN'T HOLD HIM DOWN, BECAUSE HE'S GOD, AND ALSO TO PROVE THAT HE'D BEEN SUCCESSFUL. OH YES, AND ALSO BECAUSE HE NEEDS TO BE ALIVE AND IN HEAVEN TO WELCOME THOSE OF US WHO FOLLOW HIM.

Thanks Professor Tanktop. Hope that helped.

Did You Know?

The reason that Christians (people who follow Jesus) have Sunday as the first day of the week is to remember when Jesus came back to life...on a **Sunday**.

Easter Egg Rolling

Rolling eggs downhill at Easter seems a strange way to pass the time especially as there's every chance of the eggs breaking aong the way.

AFTER ALL THE TROUBLE WE'VE GONE TO LAY THEM, IT'S VERY THOUGHTLESS!

So why do we do it then?

Eggs are seen as a symbol of the **stone being rolled away from the tomb** where Jesus was laid, it's as simple as that. The rules of an **Easter Egg Roll** are simply to see who can roll their egg the furthest distance (or can roll their egg without breaking it) down a hill (preferably a grass one).

BORING BIBLE!
EASTER LAUGHS

**Why did the
Easter egg hide?**

Because he was a
little chicken!

What did the man say when he saw ten Easter Bunnies hopping
over the hill?
There go ten Easter Bunnies hopping over the hill!

What's the best way to send a letter to the Easter Bunny?
Hare mail!

Why did the Easter Bunny cross the road?
Because the chicken had his Easter Eggs!

Why shoudn't you tell an Easter egg a joke?

Because it might crack up!

What do you call an Easter Bunny on a farm?
Dinner!

What's the difference between a crazy bunny and a counterfeit note?
One is bad money and the other is a mad bunny!

What did the man say when he saw ten Easter Bunnies hopping over the hill wearing sunglasses?
Nothing - he didn't recognise them!

How do Easter Bunnies stay healthy?

Eggs-ercise!

Why are people always tired in April?
Because they've just finished a March!

What do you call ten Easter Bunnies marching backwards?
A receding hareline!

How many Easter eggs can you put into an empty Easter basket?
One. After that the basket won't be empty!

Why do Easter eggs go to school?
To get an egg-ucation!

Why must carrots be
good for your eyes?

**Because you never
see a rabbit
wearing glasses!**

When does Valentine's Day come after Easter?
In a dictionary!

What do you get if you pour hot water into a rabbit hole?
Hot cross bunnies!
(But DON'T!!!)

Why can't the Easter Bunny's nose be twelve inches long?

Because then it would be a foot!

What did you think of these Easter jokes?
Eggs-cellent! (I hope).

Some *Un*-boring Bible Bits About Easter - Number Eleven....

ALIVE AND KICKING!

'It was late that **Sunday evening**, and the disciples were gathered together behind locked doors, because they were afraid of the Jewish authorities. Then **Jesus came and stood among them**...

After saying this, he showed them his **hands** and his **side**. The disciples were **filled with joy** at seeing the Lord. Jesus said to them again, "Peace be with you. As the Father sent me, so I send you."

Then he breathed on them and said, "**Receive the Holy Spirit**. If you forgive people's sins, they are forgiven; if you do not forgive them, they are not forgiven."

One of the twelve disciples, **Thomas** (called the Twin), was not with them when Jesus came.

So the other disciples told him, "We have seen the Lord!"

Thomas said to them, "Unless I see the **scars of the nails** in his hands and put my finger on those scars and my hand in his side, **I will not believe**."

A week later the disciples were together again indoors, and Thomas was with them.

The doors were locked, but Jesus came and stood among them and said, "Peace be with you."

Then he said to Thomas, "Put your finger here, and look at my hands; then stretch out your hand and put it in my side. Stop your doubting, and believe!"

Thomas answered him...

Jesus said to him, "Do you believe because you see me? How happy are those who believe *without* seeing me!" '

A snatch from Bible book **John**, chapter 20 and verses 19 to 29.

Fascinating Fact:

**Did you know that the Bible tells us
that after his resurrection from the dead,
Jesus appeared to his disciples (and other people
who'd known him before his death) on many occasions.
In fact, we're even told that he showed himself
to a crowd of 500 of his followers in one hit.
These appearances lasted for 40 days.**

I suppose he *could* have done but if he *had*, the second part of his **rescue plan** for the human race wouldn't have been accomplished.

Jesus was only on a **flying visit** to Planet Earth (what's 33 years by comparison with the whole of eternity?) simply to do a job and then to go back home to heaven.

But that wasn't the *only* reason. Jesus *also* had one more brilliant thing up his sleeve that required his return.

Wanna know what that was?

Well, even if you *don't* I'm still going to tell you, so there!

Top of Jesus's '**To Do**' list had been to get that whole **sin business** sorted and dealt with (which he did on the cross). As we've found out from that bit about the Temple curtain being **ripped in two**, we can now approach God as his friends again (fuller details a bit later).

But now here's the rub.

It's all very well us human beings getting a **second chance** with God but if you're anything like me then you're sure to **foul up** again, sooner or later, and then we'll be back where we started. But fret not...

...God had already thought of that.

We've got one more *un*-boring Bible bit to check out which should make things a lot clearer.

Read on!

Some *Un*-boring Bible Bits About Easter - Number Twelve....

AU REVOIR!

'Dear Theophilus:

In my first book I wrote about all the things that **Jesus** did and taught from the time he began his work until the day he was taken up to heaven.

Before he was taken up, he gave instructions by the power of the Holy Spirit to the men he had chosen as his apostles.

For **40 days after his death** he appeared to them many times in ways that proved beyond doubt that **he was alive**.

They saw him, and he talked with them about the Kingdom of God.

And when they came together, he gave them this order...

When the apostles met together with Jesus, they asked him, "Lord, will you at this time give the Kingdom back to Israel?" Jesus said to them, "The times and occasions are set by my Father's own authority, and it is not for you to know when they will be".

BUT WHEN THE HOLY SPIRIT COMES UPON YOU, YOU WILL BE FILLED WITH POWER, AND YOU WILL BE WITNESSES FOR ME IN JERUSALEM, IN ALL JUDEA AND SAMARIA, AND TO THE ENDS OF THE EARTH.

After saying this, he was **taken up to heaven** as they watched him, and a cloud hid him from their sight.
They still had their eyes fixed on the sky as he went away, when **two men dressed in white** suddenly stood beside them and said, "Galileans, why are you standing there looking up at the sky? This Jesus, who was taken from you into heaven, will come back in the same way that you saw him go to heaven." '

A snatch from Bible book **Acts**, chapter 1 and verses 1 to 11.

So, did you spot Jesus's brill plan to stop us keep on fouling up?

It sure was.

Jesus needed to go back to heaven so he could send (in place of himself) the **Holy Spirit** (who is *also* God).

And here's where it gets even *cleverererer* (I think there's too many 'ers' aren't there?)

There most certainly are! - The Editor

Oops! I didn't think he was still keeping his beedy eye on things. Now where was I? Oh yes, the *clever* bit.

When *we* have got the **Holy Spirit** living inside of us (like Jesus did) then we can do the same sort of things that *he* did.

Er, no. But it *does* mean that the Holy Spirit can help us live good lives which make God happy.

All you need to know is that one day (some time in the future, only *God* knows when) Jesus is going to **come back to this planet** to collect every one of us who's taken up his offer to be friends with God.

Because the world we live in has being **spoiled** by the knock-on effects of all that **sin**, God's plan is to make a new world, but *this* time there's going to be absoulutely no chance of fouling things up.

In fact ,things are going to even *better* second time round.

I don't know about you but I reckon that booking a place there is a **pretty smart move**.

Fascinating Fact:

Did you know that the Bible not only contains ads (or prophecies) that tell the world about Jesus's first visit to Planet Earth but there's heaps and heaps of them that also either hint or tell us loud and clear that he's coming back a second time.

Which means that if the first lot of prophecies about Jesus being born as a child and dying on a cross came true (which they did) then we can be sure that all the ads about him coming back at the end of time are gonna happen as well.

In a bit I'm going to tell you how to go about making sure you're **100% sorted with God** but *first* a bit more **Easter trivia**.

The World's Biggest Chocolate Easter Egg

The **Belgian** chocolate producer **Guylian** made a chocolate egg that shot into the record books as The World's Biggest Chocolate Easter Egg. The **beast of a feast** was made out of over **50,000 chocolate bars** and was specially commissioned by the Belgian city of St.Niklaas.

The egg measured **8.32 metres high** and beats the record of Kwazulu-Natal in South-Africa in 1996.

That egg was 7.65 metres high.

Twenty-six craftsman worked altogether **525 hours** to build the egg which consisted of **1950 kg** of chocolates.

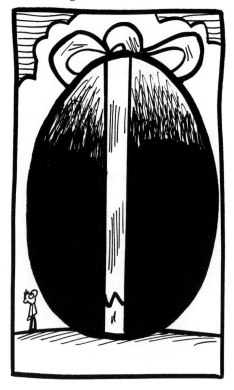

Alderman Urbain Vercauteren of the city of St.Niklaas is quoted as saying that the egg wasn't meant to be eaten.

"After a week outside in all weather conditions, I don't think it would be very tasteful."

Good point!

The World's Biggest Inedible Easter Egg

If you travel to **Vegreville** in Canada (that's unless you happen to live there already, in which case you dont need to travel *anywhere*!) you can see the **World's Biggest Inedible Easter Egg** (that means you can't eat it - sorry). Why make a monster of an egg that you *can't* tuck into? Well, the Easter egg or Ukranian '**Pysanka**', was built (in 1975) to commemorate early Ukranian settlements in an area east of Edmonton (Canada).

The Pysanka is basically a **whopping great jigsaw puzzle** made up of 524 star patterns, 2,206 equilateral triangles, 3,512 visible facets, 6,978 nuts and bolts, and 177 internal struts. It measures 25.7 feet long, 18.3 feet wide, **stands 31.6 feet high** and weighs a hefty 5,000 pounds. The whole thing took 12,000 man hours to construct and it even turns like a weather vane.

Who takes credit for this record breaking egg?

Take a bow, **Professor Ronald Resch**, a computer scientist at the University of Utah

Did You Know?

That an ostrich egg (at **3.3 pounds**) is the **world's largest egg**.
Some dinosaurs laid even *larger* eggs.
and you can check out evidence of this fact in the American Museum of Natural History (in New York) where they've got a dinosaur egg that's about the size of **basketball**!

When it comes to the *other* end of the scale the smallest bird egg in the world is that of the **bee hummingbird**.
You could put **4,700** bee hummingbird eggs inside **one** ostrich egg.
The bee hummingbird egg is the size of a small pea and weighs only **.02 ounces**.

Real Life Stories of People Who Had Their Lives Changed by Jesus

Abraham Lincoln

Abraham Lincoln has gone down in history as one of America's greatest presidents. He was born in **Kentucky** (in 1809) and grew up as someone who built his life on the teaching of the **Bible**. This was thanks to his mother (Nancy) who died when he was young and to his stepmother (Sarah Bush). Lincoln is on record as saying that the Bible helped him know the difference between right and wrong.

Despite his Christian upbringing, Lincoln (now a lawyer) wasn't actually a Christian himself even though he thought the Bible was a **good book**.

Everything changed following the **death of his son**, Willie, Abraham Lincoln suddenly understood that he could have a real, **one-to-one relationship with Jesus**.

Because *he'd* received God's forgiveness, Lincoln dedicated his life to bringing peace and reconcilliation to his war-torn country.

Amy Carmichael

Amy Carmichael was born in **Northern Ireland** (in 1867), the oldest of seven children. The death of her father while she was still a teenager had a big effect on her and made her think long and hard about where her life was heading and what God had lined up for her.

One year later she found herself at a Christian meeting in England's Lake District where she came to the conclusion that nothing could be more important than living her life for Jesus Christ who she knew had given His life for her.

Not only *that* but Amy was aware that Jesus was calling her to give all of herself to *back* to Him. Coming from a well-to-do family this meant giving up a lot, but she did it.

In **1895**, Amy was commissioned by the Church of England **Zenana Missionary Society** to go to Dohnavur, India, where she served for **fifty-six years**.

A big part of her work was devoted to rescuing children who temple prostitution.

If you wanted to describe Amy Carmichael's life you'd use words like obedience, commitment,and selflessness.

Here was a woman who a risen Jesus had used amazingly.

David Berkowitz

From childhood David Berkowitz's life was **tough**. He was a very **mixed up child** and by the time he reached his teenage years things had gone from **bad to worse**. Following the early death of his mother he inlisted in the US Army but on his return to civilian life in New York he started to get in with the wrong crowd. The people he was spending his time with didn't worship Jesus - they worshipped his No.1 enemy, the devil.

It's no surprise that living life on the dark side led to him committing six horrific murders for which he received a life prison sentence.

Ten years into his life sentence David became depressed but things were about to change. A fellow inmate (a Christian) told him that Jesus can forgive *anyone* (however bad they are). After reading the Bible, David Berkowitz turned his back on his evil past and handed his life over to Jesus.

A wonderful peace filled David's heart like he'd never known before.

Since that day, David Berkowitz has been a changed man and he has given his life to telling fellow prisoners (and the world at large) that Jesus can change *their* lives as well.

Henrietta Mears

Henrietta was born in Fargo, **North Dakota**, USA in **1890** and she became a follower of Jesus early in her life thanks to her mum's example.

Teaching and education was her passion and before long Henrietta was director of Christian Education at First Presbysterian Church in **Hollywood** where the Sunday School attendance went through the roof as a result of her efforts.

But when Henrietta discovered that the Sunday School material she was expected to use **watered down** the Bible she decided to write her *own*. It was *so* popular that in due course **Gospel Light** publishers was formed to cope with the demand for it.

When Henrietta needed $350,000 for a Christian retreat she simply **asked God** for it and **believed** he'd come up with the goods, which he did but for an amazing knock-down price of only **$30,000**.

Henrietta Mears was a woman who believed God **wholeheartedly** and as a result saw God do **great things** through her.

Now *there's* and example to follow!

If you want to find out loads *more* info about how Jesus is **changing lives** and what he's been doing since he went back home to heaven then why not buy yourself a copy of either Boring Bible book *Saints Alive* or *Crazy Christians* (or *both* if you're loaded).

If ever anyone needed **proof** that Jesus is still **alive and kicking** then stories like the ones we've just looked are brilliant evidence.

A *dead* Jesus simply couldn't do that sort of thing.

And what's more, there are *countless* people around the world who even claim to have had a **personal visit from Jesus** to prove he's alive or perhaps a **dream** where he appears to them to convince them he's **for real**.

Fascinating Fact:

Somebody has helpfully worked out that every day a staggering 174,000 people become Christians. Added to that, 3,500 new churches are started to carry on the work of telling people about Jesus.

I WISH THERE WAS AN EASIER WAY OF COUNTING THE NUMBER OF NEW CHRISTIANS!

It's nearly the end of the book but we've still got a few more things to cram in (don't say we don't give you value for money).

Cheapskate!

One of the things I *almost* forgot to include (but don't let on to the editor or he'll have my guts for garters)...

I'm going to anyway - the Editor.

...is some foody bits.

And who *better* to introduce a Boring Bible gastronomic (foody) feature than our very own Boring Bible **chef**.

One a penny...

Hot Cross buns have been a symbol of **Good Friday** for centuries.

Although nowdays you can get your hands on them nearly all year round they were *originally* baked to be eaten only on Good Friday. The icing cross symbolised the **cross of Jesus** who *died* on a Friday.

This familiar **nursery rhyme** began in England as a call of the street vendors trying to sell their wares with cries of "Hot Cross Buns! "Hot Cross Buns!"

Hot Cross Buns have not *always* been associated with Christianity. Their roots lie in pagan traditions of ancient cultures, with the cross representing the four quarters of the moon. Early Christian missionairies adopted the buns and **re-interpreted** the icing cross. In **1361**, a monk named **Father Thomas Rockcliffe** began a tradition of giving Hot Cross Buns to the poor of St Albans on Good Friday.

Ingredients:

2 packages of active dry yeast (1/4 ounce each)
1/2 cup warm water*
1 cup warm milk*
1/2 cup sugar
1/4 cup softened butter or margarine
1 teaspoon vanilla
1 teaspoon salt
1/2 teaspoon ground nutmeg
6 1/2 to 7 cups all-purpose flour
4 eggs
1/2 cup dried currants
1/2 cup raisins
----
2 tablespoons water
1 egg yolk
----
1 cup confectioner's sugar
4 teaspoons milk or cream
Dash ofsalt
1/4 teaspoon vanilla

The publishers of this book,its author and anyone even vaguely connected with the it including my pet goldfish take no responsibility whatsoever for these recipes going horribly wrong or for you feeling sick or unwell after eating the end result. Sorry, but we can't quite stretch to costly court cases for damages!

Have the water and milk at 110-115 degrees F. In a large mixing bowl, dissolve the yeast in the warm water. Add the warm milk, sugar, butter, vanilla, salt, nutmeg, and 3 cups of the flour. Beat until smooth. Add the eggs, one at a time, beating the mixture well after each addition. Stir in the dried fruit and enough flour to make a soft dough.

Turn out onto a floured surface and knead until smooth and elastic, about 6 to 8 minutes. Place in a greased bowl and turn over to grease the top. Cover with a damp towel or plastic wrap and let rise in a warm place until doubled in size (about 1 hour).

Punch the dough down and shape into 30 balls. Place on lightly greased baking sheets. Cover and let rise until doubled (about 30 minutes). Using a sharp knife, cut a cross on the top of each roll. Beat the water and egg yolk together and brush over rolls. (You will probably have more than you need, discard the unused egg glaze.) Bake at 375-degree F. for 12 to 15 minutes.

Meanwhile, make icing by combining the last four ingredients. Stir until smooth, adjusting sugar and milk to make a mixture that flows easily.

When rolls are baked, cool on wire racks. Drizzle icing over the top of each roll following the lines of the cut cross.

*1 1/2 cups warm skim milk may be substituted for the milk and water in the roll recipe above.

The Simnel Cake

Simnel cakes had been around since mediaeval times and the word simnel probably comes from the latin word '**simila**', which means fine, wheaten flour (from which the cakes were made). Different places had their own recipes but the one that gained popularity was from a place called **Shewsbury** (in England). For your info, the fourth Sunday in Lent is *still* known as **Simnel Sunday** in some places.

Simnel-style cakes are now also eaten at **Easter** when **eleven balls of marzipan** are placed around the top layer to represent the **eleven true disciples**.

Ingredients:

Almond paste:
400 g icing sugar, sifted
250 g ground almonds
1 large egg yolk, beaten lightly
3-4 tablespoons orange juice
5 drops almond essence

Cake:
250g flour
pinch salt
1 teaspoon nutmeg
1 teaspoon cinnamon
300 g currants
250 g sultanas
90 g mixed peel
160 g butter
160 g caster sugar
3 large eggs
200 ml milk to mix
(Serves 6-8)

Things you'll need: sifter, nest of bowls, food processor or electric beater, spatula, wooden spoon, 24 cm round cake tin, baking paper, brown paper and twine, rolling pin, thin metal skewer

First bit.
To make your own almond paste you will need a food processor fitted with a steel blade. Don't be tempted to use store-bought almond paste because it contains lots of sugar and few almonds, it will turn to liquid under the grill. Place icing sugar and almonds in food processor bowl. Process, slowly dripping in egg

yolk, orange juice and almond essence. The mixture should form a pliable paste. Set aside a small portion for balls with which to decorate the cake.

Second bit.
Use a sturdy non-stick cake tub or line the buttered base with baking paper. As the baking period is long (1-1 1/2 hours), prevent the cake drying out by wrapping a double thickness of brown paper around the pan and securing it with twine. Preheat oven to 160 C. Sift flour, salt and spices together, then stir in fruit and peel. Cream butter and sugar thoroughly until light and creamy then beat in eggs one at a time, until the mixture is fluffy. (Reserve a drop of egg yolk for brushing over top layer of almond paste.)Stir flour and fruit into creamed mixture (you may need to add a little milk to give the mixture a dropping consistency).

Third bit.
Place half the mixture into a greased and lined cake tin. Place the round of almond paste over the top. Cover with remaining cake mixture. Before baking the cake, give the pan of mixture a sharp tap on to a firm surface. This settles the mixture and prevents holes from forming in the cake. Bake in the centre of the oven for 1-1 1/4 hours or until a thin metal skewer inserted in the centre of the cake comes out without a trace of stickiness. Turn out cake on to a wire rack. Peel off paper and leave to cool. Level the cake by placing a weighted plate on top of the cooked cake while it is still hot.

Final bit.
Break off a third of the remaining paste and roll into a circle which is the approximate size of the tin. Set aside. Cover the top of the cake with a second round of almond paste. Roll 11 small balls of paste and place evenly around the top of the cake.

Brush the top with a little beaten egg and very lightly brown under the grill until the almond paste turns light golden brown. Remove and leave to cool.

With only six more pages remaining of the **best Easter book you've have clapped eyes on** (even though I *do* say so myself and I'm allowed to 'cos **I wrote it**!) it's time to round things up. We've checked out loads and loads of stuff about Easter, its **traditions**, its **history** and, of course, a huge dollop of info about **Jesus** and how exactly *he* fits into this festival.

What *about* the Easter Bunny?

I suppose you've got a point.

In fact, the Easter Bunny and all the other stuff connected with him is a bit like the way the **Santa Claus** and **Christmas** seem to go together.

But if you read Boring Bible book *Crackers Christmas* you'll very soon discover that **Santa Claus** has as little to do with what Christmas is *really* all about (Jesus coming to live on Planet Earth) as the **Easter Bunny** has to do with what Easter is *really* all about.

And the reason I *say* that is that the Easter Bunny might be all **cute and cuddly**...

But when it comes to getting things **patched up between you and God** the Easter Bunny can't do a single thing!

So, if what we've checked out in this book about **Jesus** and **Easter** makes sense and you want to take up God's offer of getting **all that grotty sin in your life trashed** and you want to have a **clean slate with God** then here's what you've gotta do.

First off, you need to say the **world's biggest sorry** to God.

(That means saying it as if you really *mean* it).

Next up, you've gotta make a **whopper of a decision** that you don't want to do things that are wrong (in God's eyes) **ever again**. (The Bible calls that **repentance**).

Now take it from me - you *will*. That's not to say that you should *try* to be bad it's just that **it takes time** to get to be like **Jesus** (perfect). Once God comes to live in you things will be a lot easier and you'll even find that doing wrong things actually makes you feel uncomfortable and you'll want to say "sorry" to God, pronto! But rest easy, once you've got things sorted with God and you and him are best buddies, **nothing can break that friendship**.

Then comes another biggie 'cos if you want God to be **No.1 in your life** (which is what this is all about) then you're gonna need to hand over your life to God, lock, stock and barrel (that's another way of saying **all of it**).

Making **God No.1** simply means always letting what God wants for your life be **top of the list** but, like I said, when you've got the Holy Spirit living in you that's not hard at all.

And last, but *not* least, believe with all your heart what God says - that when you've done all that he really *has* forgiven you and you really *have* got a new life with him.

It's as easy as that!

If you want to talk to God about what I've just said then take a look at the **prayer** on the next page and if you want to become a follower of Jesus (a **Christian**) then read it out to God as if you **really mean it**.

(And yes, God *can* hear you - even all the way from heaven!)

Here's a prayer you could pray to God...

> GOD, I'M REALLY SORRY FOR DOING WRONG. PLEASE FORGIVE ME AND HELP ME TO LIVE THE SORT OF LIFE THAT MAKES YOU HAPPY.
> I HAND OVER MY LIFE TO YOU, JESUS AND THANK YOU THAT YOU ARE GOING TO LIVE IN ME AND WILL NEVER, EVER LEAVE ME. AMEN

There's *loads* more stuff you need to know about **living your life for Jesus** so you'll probably need to persuade your parents to buy you Boring Bible books *Crazy Christians* and *Saints Alive!* or, failing that, fork out for them yourself!

And that brings us to the end of the book.

Hope you enjoyed it and it's given you a better idea what Easter is all about.

I wonder if it'll change anything for the Easter Bunny?

> AFTER WHAT YOU'VE SAID IT DOESN'T LOOK LIKE THERE'S MUCH OF A FUTURE FOR ME WITH EASTER!